An essential Bubblegum™ guide

Ged Backland and Phil Renshaw

You're too damn smooth for anything
no time for sleep or food
You swan around just being you
the coolest ever dude!

Cool Dude

Cool Dude is the hippest bloke around. He's cooler than a penguin in a fridge. Trademark shades and goatee beard make this dude a distinctive purveyor of cool. He can be found sampling the jazz vibes at the record store. If you need advice on anything cool or trendy then Cool Dude is the bloke to see. To be one of the 'in-crowd' then Cool Dude is the bloke to be seen with!

Most Likely to Say... Yeah, whatever!

Most Likely to Be... Listening to sounds or chillin' out in a cafe

Fave Colour Ice Blue

Bestest Mates with...

WAAAAAAAA

When things are going ga-ga
mad and not too brill
Loopy Lasses dash about
Cool Dudes they just chill.

When Nutty Tart is strutting her stuff
in a big mad floppy hat
Cool Dude's hangin' with the lads
he's far too cool for that!

When Gym Queen works out like mad
and runs on the fitness machines
Cool Dude looks on,
thinks 'that's hard work'
and chills with cool magazines.

Cool Stuff

Cola
Diet

When Sun Junkie bakes on the beach
sipping her diet lemonades
Cool Dude sits with a T-shirt on
looking all cool in his shades.

Diamond Geezer's a great bloke
but what really makes him sick
Is all the really gorgeous babes
want to be Cool Dude's chick!

Groovy Chick is Miss Popular
everyone thinks she's great
But surprise surprise, it's Cool Dude
who's her bestest mate.

Curry Monster gets a bit miffed
when his mouth is fire-filled
And Cool Dude who's eaten just the same
sits there totally chilled.

Boom Boom Boom Boom Boom Boom Boom Boom Boom Boom Boom Boom Boom Boom
Bubblegum
5PEEDI

Boy Racer wonders why Cool Dude
whose car was really cheap
Looks miles cooler than the Boy
in a clapped-out rusty heap.

Shoe Queen spends a million quid
and has every pair there is
Cool Dude just spends thirty
and still looks the flippin' biz.

Easy is real laid-back
full of peace and love
Which is why he thinks of Cool Dude
as his bestest bruv.

£300

Designer Diva wears all the labels

pays squillions for a skirt

She wonders how Cool Dude

looks so good

in combats and T-shirt.

Drama Queen's proper loopy
she's always mad and loud
Yet Cool Dude gets all the looks
in any flippin' crowd!

Footy Nutty's soccer mad
and plays with Cool Dude a lot
But it's Cool Dude who takes the penalties
coolly scoring from the spot!

Veggie loves Cool Dude to come 'round

for a monster slap-up feed

Cool Dude who's a mate,

says "it's great"

though it tastes like budgie seed!

Soya

So there you have it, it's all very clear
The low-down on the Dude is here.

If it all sounds familiar, if it rings true
Chances are, the Cool Dude's you!